The Power and Gift of asking Questions

Introduction

" Just ask, what's the worst they can say"

On paper this could be true, if the worse they can say is no, this means you can never lose by asking. You'll only ever end up in the same position you start in, but have a lot to gain, as it could be a yes, or a maybe or a negotiation to somewhere in between.

Question? What makes me qualified to discuss this?

Answer - I have spent a considerable amount of my career working for big corporate companies with high success and experienced multiple training courses for sales and service. Some good some bad, but with a consistent theme that they all include the ability to ask questions – I am by self-admission a chatterbox however the art of communication is so much more than just noise. These courses would offer a process which incorporates different techniques but put simply the outcome is that you can ask questions in certain sequences that enables smooth conversation and information gathering that lend itself to the situation and individual in front of you. Good communication is a skill that can be transferable in all aspects of life but not something we all learn about, sometimes we just learn through trial and error – the hard way!

Some questions however are expected and welcomed, due to the outcome of not asking being unacceptable. For example we wouldn't be expected to ask to go to the toilet in the workplace would we? And there are typically signposts with writing and images for toilets in most public places. At business meetings these types of questions are usually addressed as "housekeeping" and are covered off as an introduction to prevent them needing to be asked at all.

Question is: If all outcomes of asking a question leave you in no worse a situation than when you are at the start, what's stopping you?

Answer - Reality isn't on paper is it! there are emotions and feelings that come into play…

There is the common phrase "there's no such thing as a silly question" I say this all the time when I am trying to make someone feel comfortable to ask and learn and create a safe open environment to ask whatever they need to whatever that may be. However its vocabulary leans to a key driver of why I believe questions are avoided or just not asked.

This key driver is Fear – Fear of sounding silly, fear of being judged, fear of being teased, fear of embarrassment, fear of being found out, fear of sharing, fear of being vulnerable / showing vulnerability, fear of insecurities that niggle away sometimes not even consciously, until we really think about it and ask ourselves what it is we fear will happen to us, if we ask that question.

The opposite key driver is Love – Love of learning, love of understanding, love of curiosity and the outcome, love of the goal or achieving the goal that will drive us to ask

Understand the power of asking a question

Learn how... Don't be shy...And no it's not rude...

Whether you're a student a stay at home Mom, entrepreneur, Mumtrepreneur, sales person, sales rep, corporate leader, or freelancer, and at any age or stage

of your life journey, this book provides an understanding of the types of

questions we can have as tools and when to use them to acheive the desired

goals that we desire.

Key benefit #1

Recognising the simple and yet huge power that asking a question can give

Key benefit #2

Understand there are different types of questions

Key benefit #3

When to use different question types appropriately

With the most impact for success

Key benefit #4

Having the confidence to just ask...

Go get started...

Chapter 1: The Power of Inquiry: Why Questions Matter

Asking questions is one of the most natural and fundamental skills we possess as human beings. From the time we are children, the simple act of asking "why" fuels our understanding of the world. It is how we grow, develop, evolve, and gain knowledge. But beyond just satisfying curiosity, questions have a much deeper power. They are the engine of communication, connection, innovation, and problem-solving.

Questions as a Tool for Understanding

At its core, a question is an invitation to learn. Whether we're engaging in a casual conversation or participating in a formal debate, questions drive the exchange of information. A well-timed or thoughtfully phrased question can unlock insights that would have otherwise remained hidden. When we ask questions, we signal an openness to listen, to understand, and to engage with another perspective.

In education, the best teachers know that teaching is less about providing answers and more about sparking the right questions in students. This approach stimulates critical thinking, pushing learners to explore beyond surface-level facts and develop a deeper, more intricate understanding of the material.

The Role of Questions in Problem-Solving

Innovation and problem-solving both thrive on inquiry. The most successful entrepreneurs, scientists, and thinkers often start with a question: "What if?" or "Why not?" They refuse to accept things at face value, instead challenging the status quo and looking for alternative solutions.

Take the invention of the airplane. The Wright brothers didn't simply accept that humans couldn't fly. They asked, "What would it take to make flight possible?" By relentlessly pursuing that question, they revolutionized transportation and forever changed the world. In much the same way, many breakthroughs in science, medicine, and technology have emerged from individuals and teams who dared to ask questions that seemed, at first, impossible.

The Power of a Well-Timed Question

In business, leadership, and negotiation, questions are tools of influence. Leaders often use questions not just to gather information, but to guide discussions, shift perspectives, or reveal underlying issues. A strategic question can be more powerful than a direct statement, prompting reflection or revealing assumptions that otherwise might go unnoticed.

In negotiations, for example, asking, "What would a perfect solution look like for you?" can lead to creative compromises and mutual understanding that might have been missed through assertive demands. A simple "Why do you think this approach is best?" can prompt someone to re-examine their stance, possibly uncovering weak points in their argument.

Questions Build Relationships

Questions aren't just tools for learning; they are also key to building meaningful relationships. In social settings, the questions we ask reveal our interest in others, showing that we care about their thoughts, experiences, and emotions. When people feel heard, they open up more, creating opportunities for genuine connection.

For example, consider how a simple "How are you?" can either open a gateway to deeper conversation or serve as a throwaway phrase, depending on how it's asked. If it's accompanied by eye contact and genuine curiosity, the same question can make someone feel seen and valued. In contrast, a hurried or distracted "How are you?" can come across as perfunctory, even if the words themselves are the same.

The Art of Asking the Right Question

However, not all questions are equal. The art lies in knowing what to ask and when. A poorly phrased question can lead to misunderstanding or defensiveness, while a powerful question can break through barriers and lead to breakthroughs.

One of the most common mistakes people make is asking questions that are too narrow or closed. These limit the response to simple yes/no answers or rote facts. In contrast, open-ended questions invite elaboration, allowing the person being asked to explore their thoughts more deeply. Compare "Did you like the presentation?" with "What stood out to you in the presentation?" The first question requires minimal thought; the second opens the door for a more detailed and insightful response.

Why We Should Question More

Despite the immense power of questions, many of us don't ask enough of them. We often fall into the trap of assuming we know more than we do, or we fear that asking questions might make us seem ignorant or uninformed. Yet the reality is that questions, especially thoughtful ones, demonstrate engagement, humility, and a willingness to learn.

Great leaders, innovators, and communicators are perpetual questioners. They don't shy away from uncertainty; instead, they embrace it as an opportunity to gain clarity. By asking more and better questions, they not only improve their understanding but also inspire those around them to think more deeply.

Conclusion

Questions can be described as the cornerstone of progress—whether in personal growth, social relationships, or professional development. They help us learn, connect, innovate, and solve problems. In a world that often values quick answers and instant solutions, the art of asking thoughtful, intentional questions is more important than ever. When we master the power of inquiry, we unlock new possibilities for ourselves and for the world around us.

Chapter 2: Crafting the Perfect Question: Techniques and Strategies

The ability to ask questions is fundamental, but the ability to ask *the right* questions is an art. Crafting a well-formed question can be the difference between a conversation that leads to superficial answers and one that unlocks insight, creativity, or problem-solving. Whether you're a leader, educator, negotiator, or simply someone seeking to deepen relationships, learning how to frame questions effectively is an invaluable skill.

In this chapter, we'll explore techniques and strategies to help you craft questions that are clear, impactful, and purposeful, allowing you to gather meaningful information and spark deeper thought.

The Power of Open-Ended Questions

One of the most effective tools for crafting impactful questions is understanding the distinction between open and closed questions. Closed questions usually lead to short, restricted answers such as "yes" or "no." While closed questions can be useful for specific information, they often cut off the potential for deeper exploration.

Open-ended questions, on the other hand, encourage expansive thinking. These questions invite the respondent to reflect, elaborate, and offer more considered answers. Instead of asking, "Did you enjoy the presentation?" consider asking, "What did you find most compelling about the presentation?" The second question not only invites reflection but also opens the door for unexpected insights.

Key Elements of Open-Ended Questions:

- **Start with words like "how," "what," "why," or "tell me about."**

- **Avoid binary choices.** Instead of framing questions as a choice between two options, allow room for a broader range of responses.

- **Encourage storytelling.** Invite the other person to share an experience or process rather than just facts.

The Importance of Clarity

Clarity is a hallmark of an effective question. A vague or ambiguous question can confuse the person you're speaking to, leading to unclear or irrelevant responses. When crafting a question, be as specific as possible without being overly restrictive.

Let's take an example: Instead of asking a vague question like, "Can you explain what happened during the meeting?" a more focused question might be, "Can you walk me through the key points discussed during the budget portion of the meeting?" The latter is more likely to produce a direct and clear response.

Strategies for Achieving Clarity:

- **Be concise.** Rambling questions can confuse both the questioner and the respondent. Keep your questions direct and to the point.

- **Break complex questions into parts.** If your question involves multiple layers or subjects, break it down into smaller, bite-sized pieces.

- **Avoid jargon.** Make sure your language is clear and appropriate for your audience. Don't talk in technical terms or acronyms unless you're certain the other person understands them.

The Role of Context in Questioning

Context shapes how questions are understood and answered. Tailoring your questions to the situation, the person you're speaking to, and the desired outcome is crucial for success. For example, if you're in a formal business meeting, your questions should reflect professionalism and precision, while in a casual conversation, they might be more relaxed and exploratory.

Consider how questions change based on context:

- In a **leadership setting**, a question like, "How can we improve team morale?" is forward-looking and is solution-oriented, suggesting that you value team input and inviting it at the same time.

- In an **educational environment**, asking, "What do you think is the most important takeaway from this lesson?" encourages critical thinking rather than memory regurgitation for the response.

- During a **personal conversation**, a question like, "How are you really feeling about this situation?" can demonstrate empathy and invite emotional openness.

Balancing Directness and Diplomacy

Not all questions are easy to ask. Some conversations require a delicate balance between getting to the heart of the matter and maintaining sensitivity. In these situations, the way a question is phrased can make all the difference.

For instance, if you're giving feedback, instead of asking, "Why did you do that wrong?" which may put someone on the defensive, you could ask, "Can you help me understand your thought process behind this decision?" This shifts the tone from blame to understanding, encouraging a more open and productive dialogue.

Techniques for Asking Sensitive Questions:

- **Use neutral language.** Avoid words that sound accusatory or judgmental which can be received as inflammatory. Phrases like "I'm curious about" or "Can you help me understand" soften the approach.

- **Give context.** If you're asking about a potentially sensitive issue, briefly explain why you're asking to immediately address with the aim to extinguish any potential feelings of ambush or defensiveness.

- **Allow space for reflection.** Instead of demanding an immediate answer, give the person time to think and offer timescales. This can be particularly useful when dealing with emotional or complex topics.

The Power of Follow-Up Questions

Often, the real value of a question isn't found in the initial inquiry but in the **follow-up**. Follow-up questions show that you're actively listening and are interested in diving deeper into the topic. They allow you to explore beyond surface-level answers and uncover additional layers of meaning.

For example, after asking, "What did you enjoy about the project?" a powerful follow-up might be, "What specific challenges did you face, and how did you overcome them?" This second question not only keeps the conversation going but also encourages a more detailed and thoughtful response.

Effective Follow-Up Strategies:

- **Probe for clarification.** If an answer is unclear or too vague, ask the person to elaborate. For instance, "Can you explain what you mean by that?"

- **Explore underlying causes.** Dig deeper by asking, "Why do you think that happened?" or "What led you to that conclusion?"

- **Acknowledge the answer before following up.** Showing that you've heard their response before asking more questions creates a feeling of respect and engagement. For example, "That's interesting. Can you tell me more about how you reached that decision?"

Avoiding Leading Questions

A common pitfall when crafting questions is unintentionally leading the respondent. **Leading questions** subtly influence the answer by suggesting a particular response or by embedding assumptions within the question itself. For example, "Don't you think this new policy is better than the old one?" assumes agreement and steers the conversation in a specific direction.

To avoid leading questions:

- **Keep your questions neutral.** Instead of asking, "Wouldn't you agree that the project was a success?" ask, "How do you feel the project went?"

- **Be mindful of tone.** Sometimes, the way a question is asked—through tone, emphasis, or body language—can lead the respondent toward a particular answer.

- **Avoid assumptions.** Don't embed your own conclusions into the question. Instead of asking, "Why did you decide to do X?" ask, "What led you to your decision?"

Conclusion: The Art of Intentional Questioning

The perfect question is one that serves a clear purpose, invites thoughtful reflection, and is sensitive to the context in which it's asked. Whether you're seeking to understand a problem, spark creativity, or deepen a relationship, crafting effective questions is about being intentional. By refining your questioning skills—using clarity, openness, context, and empathy—you can transform how you engage with others and unlock deeper insights, solutions, and connections.

Ultimately, the art of crafting questions isn't just about gathering information; it's about creating an environment where real understanding can flourish.

Chapter 3: Open vs. Closed Questions: When and How to Use Them

In conversations, meetings, interviews, and negotiations, the type of question you ask shapes the entire flow of communication. Two primary categories of questions, **open** and **closed**, serve different purposes and elicit different types of responses. Understanding when and how to use each type is key to mastering the art of inquiry.

We have already looked at the power of an open ended question but lets look at when and how to use them and their counterpart which is the closed question.

In this chapter, we will explore the characteristics, benefits, and potential drawbacks of open and closed questions, as well as when each type is most effective. By understanding how to leverage both, you'll be better equipped to steer conversations, gather information, and build meaningful dialogues.

What Are Closed Questions?

Closed questions are typically short, direct questions that limit responses to a finite set of answers, often "yes" or "no," or a specific piece of information. These questions are ideal when you need to confirm facts, clarify details, or gain quick answers. They help you stay focused on specific points and are useful in situations where time is limited or precision is necessary.

Examples of closed questions:

- "Did you attend the meeting?"
- "Is the project on schedule?"
- "What time did the event start?"

These questions require minimal thought and often serve as a way to gather or confirm straightforward information.

Benefits of Closed Questions

- Efficiency: Closed questions are quick to ask and answer, making them useful in fast-paced conversations or when you need to gather basic facts quickly.
- Clarity: When seeking specific details or clarifications, closed questions help avoid ambiguity. You can get the exact information you need without any unnecessary elaboration.
- Control: Closed questions allow the questioner to control the direction of the conversation by limiting the range of possible responses.
- Decision-making: In high-pressure situations, closed questions can prompt immediate decisions. For instance, "Can we move forward with this plan?" requires a direct response and helps progress toward action.

Drawbacks of Closed Questions

While closed questions have their advantages, they can also limit deeper exploration or restrict the flow of conversation. Over-reliance on them may cause interactions to feel mechanical or superficial.

- Limited insight: Closed questions often don't provide the depth needed for understanding motivations, emotions, or complex issues.
- Restricted dialogue: These questions can stifle conversation, leading to abrupt pauses or dead ends in discussions.
- Missed opportunities: You might miss valuable insights that would emerge from more open-ended inquiry.

Open questions invite a broad range of responses, encouraging deeper reflection and elaboration. Instead of restricting answers to "yes" or "no," open questions stimulate dialogue by allowing the respondent to share thoughts, feelings, or explanations. These questions are ideal for sparking discussion, uncovering underlying issues, and encouraging creativity or insight.

Examples of open questions:

- "What did you think about the meeting?"
- "How do you feel the project is progressing?"

- "Can you describe what happened at the event?"

By prompting a wider range of responses, open questions help to explore ideas and opinions in greater detail.

Benefits of Open Questions

- Encourages reflection: Open questions give people the opportunity to think about their answers, often leading to richer and more meaningful responses.
- Creates dialogue: These questions encourage conversation, often leading to more in-depth discussions and the discovery of new insights.
- Explores emotions and opinions: Open questions are especially useful for understanding someone's feelings, motivations, or perspectives.
- Stimulates creativity: In brainstorming sessions or problem-solving scenarios, open questions can spark new ideas or solutions.

Drawbacks of Open Questions

While open questions are essential for attaining deeper understanding, they do have some potential drawbacks, especially in situations where time or focus is limited.

- Time-consuming: Because they encourage elaborate responses, open questions can lead to longer, more detailed answers, which may not be ideal in time-sensitive situations.
- Potential for tangents: Open questions can sometimes lead the conversation off course, especially if the respondent interprets the question too broadly or introduces unrelated topics.
- Overwhelming for some respondents: Not everyone is comfortable or adept at providing detailed answers, which could lead to frustration or hesitation.

When to Use Closed Questions

Closed questions are especially useful when you need clear, concise information or when you want to narrow the focus of the conversation. Here are some scenarios where closed questions are particularly effective:

1. Clarifying Information

When you need to verify details or confirm facts, closed questions are perfect. For example, in a meeting, you might ask, "Is the deadline set for Friday?" This allows you to confirm a specific piece of information without ambiguity.

2. Making Quick Decisions

In decision-making scenarios, closed questions can help to quickly resolve issues or move things forward. For instance, "Can we approve this budget?" requires a simple yes/no answer, moving the conversation toward a decision.

3. Evaluating Options

When comparing options or choices, closed questions help focus the discussion. For example, "Do you prefer the first or second design?" narrows the response to a choice between two options, helping to streamline decision-making.

4. Focusing the Conversation

If the conversation starts to wander or go off-topic, closed questions can help bring it back on track. For example, "Is this relevant to the current project?" helps refocus the dialogue on the task at hand.

When to Use Open Questions

Open questions are invaluable when you want to dive deeper into a topic, encourage dialogue, or explore someone's opinions and emotions. Here are some scenarios where open questions shine:

1. Exploring Ideas or Problems

When you need to understand someone's thought process, open questions like "What do you think are the biggest challenges?" or "How can we approach this issue differently?" can stimulate broader discussion and lead to creative problem-solving.

2. Encouraging Reflection

Open questions are perfect for encouraging introspection or personal reflection. In coaching or mentorship, for instance, questions like "What have you learned from this experience?" invite the other person to explore their own growth and understanding.

3. Building Relationships

In personal or professional relationships, open questions are a powerful way to show interest and encourage deeper connection. For example, "How did you feel about the outcome?" invites the person to share their emotions and thoughts, fostering a more meaningful dialogue.

4. Gathering Insight and Feedback

When you need feedback or insight, open questions provide a platform for detailed responses. For instance, in a performance review, asking "What do you think went well this year?" invites the person to offer a thoughtful evaluation rather than a simple yes or no.

Combining Open and Closed Questions

The true art of asking questions lies in knowing how to combine both open and closed questions for a balanced conversation. Here's how to blend the two effectively:

1. Start Broad, Then Narrow

Often, the most productive conversations start with open questions and move toward more focused, closed questions. For example, you might begin with, "What challenges are you facing in this project?" to explore the broader context, followed by a closed question like, "Is the timeline the main issue?" to clarify a specific point.

2. Use Closed Questions to Clarify

After a detailed response to an open question, closed questions can help clarify specific details. For instance, if someone answers an open question about a project's progress, you could follow up with, "So, will the deadline be met?" to confirm a specific outcome.

3. Follow-Up with Open Questions

Once you've gathered the necessary facts through closed questions, open questions can help explore the implications or broader perspectives. After asking, "Is the event happening next month?" you might follow up with, "What are your expectations for its success?" to deepen the conversation.

Conclusion: Mastering the Balance

Knowing when and how to use open and closed questions is essential for effective communication. Closed questions give you the clarity and precision you need to confirm facts and make quick decisions, while open questions foster exploration, dialogue, and deeper understanding.

By mastering both types of questions and learning to blend them effectively, you can guide conversations toward your desired outcome while keeping them engaging and meaningful. Whether you're leading a team, building relationships, or solving complex problems, the strategic use of open and closed questions will empower you to navigate any dialogue with confidence and purpose.

Chapter 4: The Listening Mindset: Understanding Before Asking

In the art of asking questions, listening plays a pivotal role. Before we even think about what to ask, we must first engage in deep, attentive listening. This allows us to truly understand the person, situation, or context, and shapes the quality of the questions we ask. When we adopt a *listening mindset*, we not only gain richer insights, but we also build trust, foster empathy, and create stronger, more meaningful connections.

This chapter delves into the principles and techniques behind the listening mindset and explores why understanding before asking is critical for effective communication.

Why Listening Matters

At its core, listening is more than just hearing words. It is an active, deliberate process of interpreting and understanding what is being said—both verbally and non-verbally. When we listen well, we gain deeper insights into the speaker's intentions, emotions, and needs. This allows us to ask more thoughtful, relevant questions and opens the door to more productive and meaningful conversations.

Here's why listening is essential before asking questions:

- **Informed questioning:** When we take the time to listen, we can ask better, more relevant questions. Instead of generic or surface-level inquiries, we can focus on the specific issues, concerns, or topics that truly matter to the other person.

- **Building trust:** Active listening signals to the speaker that we value their perspective. When someone feels heard, they are more likely to open up, share more information, and engage in deeper conversations.

- **Preventing misunderstandings:** Many misunderstandings stem from poor listening. By truly understanding the other person's message, we reduce the risk of misinterpretation and ensure that our questions are aligned with their needs.

The Components of Active Listening

To fully embrace a listening mindset, we need to practice **active listening**. Active listening goes beyond passive hearing and involves being fully present in the moment, paying attention to both the words and the emotions behind them. Here are the key components:

1. Presence

Being present means giving your full attention to the speaker without distractions. This involves setting aside your own thoughts, judgments, and preconceptions and focusing entirely on what the other person is saying. Avoid multitasking, thinking about your next response, or interrupting.

- **Tip:** Use non-verbal cues like nodding, maintaining eye contact, and leaning in slightly to show that you are engaged in the conversation.

2. Non-Verbal Listening

Often, what is unsaid carries more weight than the actual words. Body language, tone of voice, facial expressions, and gestures can provide valuable insight into how the speaker truly feels. By paying attention to these cues, you gain a fuller understanding of the message being conveyed.

- **Tip:** Watch for inconsistencies between words and body language. For example, someone may say they are "fine" while their crossed arms and downcast eyes suggest otherwise. This can inform the questions you ask to explore their true feelings.

3. Empathy

Empathetic listening means putting yourself in the speaker's shoes. It involves not just understanding their words, but also their emotions, motivations, and experiences. When you listen with empathy, you connect with the speaker on a deeper level and can tailor your questions to address their concerns more meaningfully.

- **Tip:** Use empathetic statements such as, "I understand that this must have been challenging for you" or "It sounds like you're feeling frustrated." These phrases validate the speaker's emotions and show that you are genuinely engaged in their perspective.

4. Reflection and Clarification

Active listening also involves reflecting on what the speaker has said and offering clarification to ensure you understand them correctly. This prevents assumptions and helps create an opportunity for the speaker to elaborate or correct misunderstandings.

- **Tip:** Paraphrase key points back to the speaker, using phrases like, "What I'm hearing is that you're concerned about…" or "So if I understand correctly, you're saying that…" This not only helps clarify meaning but also shows that you are paying attention.

The Benefits of Listening Before Asking

When we listen before we ask questions, we elevate the conversation and create opportunities for greater insight. Let's explore some specific benefits:

1. More Targeted Questions

When you truly understand what the other person is saying, you can ask more specific and relevant questions. Instead of asking broad, generic questions, you can delve into the most important issues or concerns. For example, instead of asking, "How was your day?" you might say, "You mentioned feeling stressed earlier—what's been weighing on your mind?"

This ability to ask targeted questions not only yields more meaningful answers but also demonstrates that you've been paying close attention.

2. Deeper Understanding

Listening first helps you gather important context that informs your questions. For example, if someone is discussing a problem at work, by actively listening, you may notice details about their emotional state or hidden frustrations that you can explore further with questions like, "What aspects of this situation are most frustrating for you?" or "How does this affect your motivation?"

The result is a more nuanced and comprehensive understanding of the issue, allowing for more thoughtful responses and solutions.

3. Building Rapport and Trust

When people feel listened to, they are more likely to open up and share more deeply. Listening before asking fosters a sense of safety and trust in the conversation. By demonstrating that you genuinely care about their perspective, the speaker will feel more comfortable being honest and vulnerable.

In professional settings, listening is an essential leadership skill. Team members who feel heard are more likely to contribute ideas, provide feedback, and collaborate. In personal relationships, active listening strengthens emotional connections, fostering intimacy and trust.

4. Reducing Bias and Prejudgment

Often, we ask questions based on our assumptions or preconceptions. Listening first helps reduce this bias by allowing us to approach the conversation with an open mind. Instead of jumping to conclusions, we base our questions on the actual information being shared, leading to more accurate and thoughtful exchanges.

For example, if someone is explaining a disagreement they had, instead of assuming who was at fault, you might ask, "What do you think led to the disagreement?" This approach is less judgmental and encourages deeper exploration of the situation.

Common Barriers to Effective Listening

Even with the best intentions, listening can be challenging. Many of us fall into certain habits that prevent us from fully engaging with the speaker. Here are some common barriers to effective listening and how to overcome them:

1. Internal Dialogue

Often, we are so focused on formulating our next response or thinking about our own perspective that we stop truly listening. This internal dialogue distracts us from the speaker's message.

- **Solution:** Practice mindfulness in conversation by focusing on the present moment. Let go of the urge to plan your response while the other person is speaking.

2. Interruptions

Interrupting the speaker breaks the flow of communication and signals that you are more interested in your own point of view than theirs.

- **Solution:** Wait until the speaker has fully finished their thought before responding. If you have an urge to interrupt, take a deep breath and allow them to complete their message first.

3. Judgment

We may be quick to judge or evaluate what the other person is saying, which can cloud our ability to listen objectively. Prejudging can lead to biased questions or dismissive responses.

- **Solution:** Approach each conversation with an open mind. Suspend judgment and allow the speaker to express their full perspective before forming your opinion.

4. Multitasking

Trying to listen while doing something else—such as checking your phone, typing an email, or thinking about your to-do list—reduces the quality of your listening.

- **Solution:** Eliminate distractions when engaging in important conversations. Put away your phone, close unnecessary tabs, and focus entirely on the speaker.

Listening to Non-Verbal Cues

In addition to listening to the speaker's words, pay attention to **non-verbal communication**, such as body language, facial expressions, and tone of voice. These signals often reveal more than the words themselves. A person's posture, gestures, and eye contact can give you clues about how they're feeling, even if they aren't saying it outright.

For example:

- A tense posture may indicate discomfort or anxiety.

- Frequent pauses or hesitations might signal uncertainty.

- A warm tone of voice could indicate enthusiasm or positivity.

When you incorporate these non-verbal cues into your understanding, you can ask more insightful follow-up questions that address both the spoken and unspoken elements of the conversation.

Conclusion: The Listening Mindset in Practice

Adopting a **listening mindset** is essential for mastering the art of asking questions. By focusing on understanding the speaker first, we can craft better, more relevant questions that lead to deeper, more meaningful conversations. Active listening isn't just a communication technique; it's a mindset that prioritizes empathy, presence, and understanding.

When we listen before asking, we create a space where both parties feel heard and valued. This lays the foundation for stronger relationships, more effective problem-solving, and richer insights. The next time you find yourself in a conversation, pause, listen carefully, and let your questions flow from a place of genuine understanding.

Chapter 5: Sparking Curiosity: Questions that Inspire Deeper Thinking

Curiosity is the engine of learning, innovation, and creativity. It's the driving force that compels us to explore the unknown, challenge assumptions, and expand our understanding of the world around us. In conversations, the right questions can ignite curiosity, spark intellectual exploration, and inspire deeper thinking. These questions encourage others to reflect more deeply, consider alternative perspectives, and think critically about issues or ideas.

In this chapter, we explore the art of crafting questions that inspire curiosity and promote deeper thought. We'll look at why curiosity matters, the types of questions that stimulate reflective thinking, and strategies to encourage curiosity-driven dialogue in both personal and professional settings.

The Power of Curiosity

Curiosity transforms passive communication into active engagement. It pushes people beyond surface-level thinking, encouraging them to explore, question, and learn. When curiosity is sparked in a conversation, it opens the door to deeper insights, more creative solutions, and greater intellectual growth.

Why curiosity matters in conversations:

- **Encourages exploration:** Curiosity-driven questions invite people to think beyond obvious answers and explore new possibilities.

- **Stimulates creativity:** These questions push individuals to consider alternative viewpoints and generate innovative ideas.

- **Develops personal growth:** By prompting reflection, curiosity questions encourage people to challenge their beliefs, assumptions, and understanding.

- **Builds engagement:** Questions that spark curiosity keep conversations lively and engaging, making the exchange of ideas more dynamic and meaningful.

Curiosity is the key to intellectual development, whether you're engaging in a casual conversation, brainstorming with a team, or mentoring someone through a challenging decision. The right question can open up a world of new ideas.

What Makes a Question Curiosity-Driven?

Not all questions are created equal when it comes to inspiring curiosity. Certain types of questions encourage deeper thought and reflection, while others may limit exploration. Curiosity-driven questions often share the following characteristics:

1. Open-Ended

Curiosity-driven questions are typically **open-ended**, meaning they don't have a simple yes or no answer. These questions invite the other person to elaborate, reflect, and share their thoughts in a more expansive way. Open-ended questions challenge the respondent to think broadly and creatively, leading to more interesting and nuanced answers.

Examples:

- "What possibilities do you see for the future of this project?"

- "How do you think this decision will affect the team in the long run?"

2. Exploratory

These questions encourage exploration and discovery. They often start with words like *how*, *why*, or *what if*, signalling that the questioner is interested in delving deeper into the subject. Exploratory questions can challenge assumptions and lead to new insights.

Examples:

- "Why do you think this issue is so important to people?"

- "What if we approached the problem from a completely different angle?"

3. Provocative

Curiosity questions are often provocative, not in a confrontational sense, but in their ability to provoke thought. They push the other person to think in ways they may not have considered before, gently nudging them outside of their comfort zone.

Examples:

- "What would you do if there were no limits to what you could achieve?"
- "How would you solve this problem if money were no object?"

4. Future-Focused

Questions that inspire curiosity often focus on the future or hypothetical scenarios. These questions encourage people to think beyond their current situation and imagine what could be. This not only sparks creativity but also helps in setting goals or imagining different outcomes.

Examples:

- "What do you think will happen if we continue on this path?"
- "What would success look like for you in five years?"

Techniques for Crafting Curiosity-Driven Questions

To inspire deeper thinking, it's important to approach questioning with intentionality. Here are some strategies to help you craft curiosity-driven questions that lead to meaningful exploration and reflection.

1. Challenge Assumptions

Many of the most thought-provoking questions challenge the assumptions that underlie a person's thinking. These questions force the other person to reconsider what they take for granted and explore alternative viewpoints or solutions.

Examples:

- "What assumptions are we making about this situation?"
- "Is there a different way to approach this that we haven't considered yet?"

Challenging assumptions can open the door to fresh insights and uncover blind spots in decision-making or problem-solving processes.

2. Encourage Critical Thinking

Curiosity-driven questions often prompt critical thinking by encouraging people to evaluate their own ideas, beliefs, or strategies. These questions can help uncover underlying motivations, biases, or flaws in reasoning.

Examples:

- "What evidence supports this conclusion, and what evidence might contradict it?"
- "How do you know that this is the best course of action?"

Encouraging critical thinking helps refine ideas, making them stronger and more grounded in reason.

3. Create Hypothetical Scenarios

Presenting hypothetical scenarios is a great way to spark curiosity and encourage someone to think about possibilities beyond their current reality. Hypothetical questions are often used in brainstorming sessions, strategic planning, or personal development conversations.

Examples:

- "What if we had to start from scratch—how would you approach this?"
- "Imagine you've already achieved your goal. What did you do to get there?"

By removing real-world constraints, hypothetical questions allow people to think freely and creatively.

4. Ask About Causes and Consequences

Understanding causes and consequences helps people think more deeply about the ripple effects of their actions, decisions, or ideas. Questions that focus on the *why* and *how* of a situation prompt reflection on deeper motivations and long-term outcomes.

Examples:

- "What do you think caused this issue to arise in the first place?"
- "How do you think this decision will affect things in the future?"

This type of questioning promotes forward-thinking and helps people anticipate both intended and unintended consequences.

5. Include Multiple Perspectives

Another way to spark curiosity is to ask questions that encourage people to consider alternative perspectives. This can help broaden their understanding of a situation and lead to more balanced, well-rounded thinking.

Examples:

- "How might someone with a completely different background view this situation?"

- "What would our competitors say if they saw our strategy?"

By inviting multiple perspectives, you encourage the person to step outside of their own viewpoint and see the issue from a new angle.

Inspiring Curiosity in Different Contexts

The art of sparking curiosity isn't limited to one-on-one conversations—it can be applied across a wide range of settings. Whether you're in a classroom, a business meeting, or a personal conversation, curiosity-driven questions can elevate the quality of discussion.

1. In the Workplace

In a business environment, curiosity-driven questions can help teams innovate, problem-solve, and strategize more effectively. By encouraging colleagues to think beyond the obvious, you create a culture of continuous improvement and creativity.

Examples:

- "What can we learn from this setback, and how can we apply those lessons moving forward?"

- "What emerging trends might disrupt our industry in the next five years?"

Such questions encourage forward-thinking, helping businesses stay agile and proactive in the face of change.

2. In Education

In the classroom, questions that inspire curiosity foster a love of learning. These questions engage students, encouraging them to think critically and explore topics in greater depth.

Examples:

- "What do you think would happen if this historical event had played out differently?"

- "How could this scientific discovery change the way we live in the future?"

Curiosity-driven questions in education cultivate intellectual curiosity, empowering students to become lifelong learners.

3. In Personal Relationships

In personal relationships, curiosity can help deepen connections and understanding. Asking curiosity-driven questions shows that you're interested in the other person's thoughts, feelings, and experiences, fostering trust and emotional intimacy.

Examples:

- "What has been on your mind lately that you haven't had a chance to talk about?"

- "If you could change one thing about the way we communicate, what would it be?"

These types of questions open the door to deeper conversations and shared insights, strengthening the relationship.

4. In Personal Growth and Development

When it comes to personal growth, curiosity-driven questions encourage self-reflection and self-awareness. These questions help individuals think deeply about their goals, values, and challenges, promoting growth and positive change.

Examples:

- "What are the beliefs that have shaped the decisions you've made?"

- "What would you pursue if you knew you couldn't fail?"

These questions encourage people to explore their inner motivations, clarify their aspirations, and take ownership of their personal development journey.

Cultivating a Curiosity Mindset

Sparking curiosity in others begins with cultivating a curiosity mindset in yourself. When you approach conversations with genuine interest and a desire to learn, you naturally ask questions that lead to deeper thinking. Here are a few tips for developing a curiosity-driven approach:

- **Stay open-minded:** Adopt a mindset of curiosity in every interaction, remaining open to new ideas, perspectives, and insights.

- **Ask with genuine interest:** Don't just ask questions to keep a conversation going; ask because you are truly interested in hearing the other person's thoughts.

- **Be willing to explore the unknown:** Curiosity requires embracing uncertainty and being comfortable not having all the answers. Don't be afraid to ask questions that lead into uncharted territory.

- **Keep an inquisitive attitude:** Approach every conversation as an opportunity to learn. Even if the topic seems familiar, there's always something new to discover.

Conclusion: Questions That Spark Curiosity

The ability to ask questions that spark curiosity is one of the most powerful tools in your communication arsenal. By crafting questions that challenge assumptions, invite exploration

Chapter 6: Navigating Difficult Conversations with Thoughtful Questions

Difficult conversations are a natural part of life, whether in personal relationships, workplaces, or social settings. These conversations might involve conflict, disagreement, or sensitive topics, making them challenging to navigate. However, asking the right questions can help diffuse tension, foster understanding, and lead to productive outcomes.

In this chapter, we explore how thoughtful, well-crafted questions can transform difficult conversations into opportunities for resolution and growth. We'll discuss the importance of empathy, the types of questions that encourage constructive dialogue, and strategies for handling sensitive topics with care and clarity.

Why Thoughtful Questions Matter in Difficult Conversations

Difficult conversations often stir strong emotions—anger, frustration, anxiety, or defensiveness. In such moments, it's easy for the conversation to spiral out of control, with both parties talking past each other or getting stuck in an argument. Thoughtful questions can help manage these emotions and keep the conversation focused on understanding and resolution.

Here's why thoughtful questions are so valuable in difficult conversations:

- **Defusing tension:** Asking a neutral or empathetic question can help calm heightened emotions and redirect the conversation toward problem-solving.

- **Encouraging openness:** Thoughtful questions signal that you're genuinely interested in the other person's perspective, which encourages them to share more openly and honestly.

- **Promoting understanding:** Asking questions that seek to understand, rather than accuse, leads to greater clarity about the issues at hand and helps avoid misunderstandings.

- **Fostering collaboration:** Thoughtful questions create a sense of collaboration, turning a potentially adversarial conversation into a joint effort to resolve the problem.

Key Principles for Asking Thoughtful Questions

Navigating a difficult conversation successfully requires emotional intelligence and careful consideration of how and when to ask questions. The following principles can help guide your approach:

1. Stay Calm and Centred

In challenging conversations, it's easy to become emotionally reactive, which can lead to defensive or aggressive questioning. Before asking questions, take a moment to centre yourself and manage your emotions. A calm, steady tone communicates that you're approaching the conversation thoughtfully rather than impulsively.

- **Tip:** If emotions are running high, take a brief pause to collect your thoughts before asking your next question.

2. Use Open-Ended Questions

Open-ended questions are particularly valuable in difficult conversations because they encourage dialogue rather than shutting it down. These questions invite the other person to elaborate on their thoughts and feelings, fostering deeper understanding. Closed questions, on the other hand, often limit the conversation to yes or no answers and can feel confrontational.

- **Open-ended example:** "Can you tell me more about what's been frustrating for you in this situation?"

- **Closed-ended example:** "Are you upset about this?"

The open-ended version invites the person to express themselves fully, while the closed-ended version may prompt a brief, non-reflective response.

3. Focus on Understanding, Not Judging

In difficult conversations, it's essential to prioritize understanding over judgment. Avoid questions that sound accusatory or judgmental, as they can put the other person on the defensive. Instead, ask questions that seek to clarify the other person's point of view.

- **Judgmental question:** "Why would you do something like that?"

- **Understanding question:** "What was your thought process behind that decision?"

The second question is more likely to elicit a thoughtful, explanatory response rather than a defensive reaction.

4. Practice Active Listening

Active listening is crucial when navigating difficult conversations. After asking a question, truly listen to the other person's response without interrupting, judging, or planning your next question. Reflect back what you've heard to ensure that you've understood correctly and show the other person that you're engaged.

- **Tip:** Use phrases like, "If I understand you correctly, you're saying…" or "It sounds like you're feeling frustrated because…" to confirm that you've accurately interpreted their words.

5. Show Empathy and Respect

Empathy is key to resolving conflict or tension. Asking questions that reflect empathy signals that you care about the other person's feelings and perspective. Even if you disagree with them, showing respect for their viewpoint builds trust and opens the door to a more constructive conversation.

- **Empathetic question:** "I can see this situation has been tough for you. Can you help me understand what's been the most challenging part?"

This question acknowledges the person's emotions while inviting them to share more.

Types of Thoughtful Questions for Difficult Conversations

Different types of questions can be used at various stages of a difficult conversation to guide it toward a positive outcome. Let's explore some of the most effective question types:

1. Clarifying Questions

In difficult conversations, misunderstandings often arise because one or both parties are unclear about the other's perspective or intentions. Clarifying questions help you gather more information and ensure that you're accurately interpreting what's being said.

Examples:

- "Can you clarify what you mean by that?"

- "When you say X, are you referring to Y?"

- "I'm not sure I fully understand your point. Could you explain that again?"

Clarifying questions prevent assumptions and ensure both parties are on the same page.

2. Exploratory Questions

These questions encourage the other person to reflect on their thoughts, feelings, or motivations. Exploratory questions are especially useful when dealing with complex emotions or underlying issues that may not be immediately apparent.

Examples:

- "What do you think might be driving these feelings?"

- "Can you explore how this situation has affected you?"

- "What do you think is at the heart of this issue?"

By encouraging the other person to explore their own emotions or reasoning, you gain deeper insight into the situation.

3. Perspective-Shifting Questions

Sometimes, difficult conversations get stuck because both parties are entrenched in their own perspectives. Perspective-shifting questions gently encourage the other person to see the situation from a different angle, fostering empathy and opening the door to new solutions.

Examples:

- "How do you think the other person might feel about this situation?"

- "What might this look like from a different perspective?"

- "If you were in my shoes, how would you approach this?"

These questions encourage empathy and can help both parties move toward mutual understanding.

4. Solution-Focused Questions

Once the core issues have been explored, solution-focused questions help steer the conversation toward resolution. These questions focus on finding common ground and generating constructive next steps.

Examples:

- "What steps do you think we can take to resolve this issue?"

- "How can we work together to improve this situation?"

- "What would a positive outcome look like for you?"

Solution-focused questions signal that you're committed to moving forward and finding a resolution that works for both parties.

5. De-Escalation Questions

In moments of heightened tension, de-escalation questions can help diffuse emotions and bring the conversation back to a calmer, more productive place. These questions focus on emotions and aim to defuse anger or frustration by acknowledging the other person's feelings.

Examples:

- "It seems like this is a really emotional issue for you—how are you feeling right now?"

- "I can tell this conversation is difficult. What can we do to make it easier to talk through this?"

- "Let's take a step back for a moment—what's the most important thing we need to focus on right now?"

By acknowledging emotions and offering a moment of calm, de-escalation questions help lower the intensity of the conversation.

Common Pitfalls to Avoid in Difficult Conversations

Even with the best intentions, it's easy to fall into certain traps during difficult conversations. Here are a few common pitfalls to watch out for, and how to avoid them:

1. Asking Leading or Loaded Questions

Leading questions are those that imply a particular answer or push the other person toward a specific conclusion. These questions can feel manipulative or accusatory and are likely to trigger defensiveness.

Leading question: "Don't you think it's obvious that this isn't working?"
Thoughtful question: "How do you feel this approach is working so far?"

To avoid leading questions, focus on open-ended, neutral language that invites honest dialogue.

2. Making Assumptions

When we assume we know what the other person is thinking or feeling, we risk miscommunication and defensiveness. Instead of assuming, ask questions that invite the other person to clarify their perspective.

- **Avoid assumption:** "I know you're upset because I didn't agree with you."

- **Ask instead:** "I get the sense that something I said might have upset you—can you share more about how you're feeling?"

Asking for clarification instead of making assumptions leads to more accurate understanding.

3. Focusing Too Much on Winning

In difficult conversations, the goal should not be to "win" but to reach mutual understanding or find a resolution. Questions that aim to prove your point or discredit the other person are counterproductive. Instead, focus on asking questions that foster collaboration.

- **Avoid:** "Don't you see that I'm right about this?"

- **Try instead:** "What do you think are the key factors we need to consider?"

Shifting the focus from winning to understanding helps build a more constructive dialogue.

Preparing for Difficult Conversations with Thoughtful Questions

Preparation is key to navigating difficult conversations with grace and clarity. Before entering into a challenging discussion, take time to reflect on your goals, emotions, and potential obstacles. Consider what questions you might ask to guide the conversation productively.

- **Clarify your goals:** What do you hope to achieve by having this conversation? Are you seeking resolution, clarity, or a change in behaviour?

- **Anticipate emotions:** Both yours and the other person's. How can you ask questions that acknowledge and accommodate for fuelled emotions both yours and the other persons

So with all things considered and what you've learnt so far...

What's stopping you asking the question. What is the worst they can say?

Printed in Great Britain
by Amazon

55519524R00030